ADDICTIONARY

ADDICTIONARY
Brave New Words

COMPILED BY **JIM BANISTER**

ILLUSTRATED BY **ROBERT HANSON**

ABRAMS IMAGE

NEW YORK

Editor: Aiah R. Wieder
Designer: Alissa Faden
Production Manager: Jacquie Poirier

Library of Congress Cataloging-in-Publication Data
Banister, Jim.
  Addictionary : brave new words [sic] / by Jim Banister.
    p. cm.
  ISBN 978-0-8109-7269-8
  1. English language—Terms and phrases—Humor. 2. English
language—Humor. 3. Vocabulary—Humor. I. Title.
  PN6231.W64B36 2008
  818.602—dc22

                        2007049006

Printed and bound in U.S.A.

10 9 8 7 6 5 4 3 2 1

Abrams Image books are available at special discounts when purchased
in quantity for premiums and promotions as well as fundraising or
educational use. Special editions can also be created to specification.
For details, contact specialmarkets@hnabooks.com or the address below.

HNA
harry n. abrams, inc.
a subsidiary of La Martinière Groupe
115 West 18th Street
New York, NY 10011
www.hnabooks.com

CONTENTS

Syllabification

Each word is divided into syllables. Determining syllable structure and word stress, while very predictable, varies across dialects and among individual speakers. No attempt has been made to account for such variance. The syllable divisons are indicated by dots. Determining the proper division follows a basic rule of "maximum onset," with the exception of double consonants, which have been split as a standard dictionary convention.

As a rule, stress is not marked except in cases where the stress contradicts that of the conventional words, roots, or morphemes that make up the word, and when the placement of stress becomes critical in maintaining the play on words that makes the words effective.

Pronunciation

Pronunciation varies in manners parallel to syllabification, with even more variance. *Addictionary* supplies pronunciations that, overall, will apply to most speakers. The typography used to indicate pronunciation has been limited to traditional character forms as much as possible. The consonants are mostly self-explanatory. The vowels show the greatest change in quality and require the use of diacritics. The more common of these diacritics will be familiar to readers, such as the marking of long vowels (e.g., the ā in late). Others may be less familiar, but the examples at right provide models for their use.

Consonants

b - as in **b**ad

ch - as in **ch**ain

d - as in **d**og

f - as in **f**ar

g - as in **g**o

h - as in **h**at

j - as in **j**oke

k - as in **k**ite

kt - as in a**ct**

l - as in **l**ook

m - as in **m**an

n - as in **n**o

ng - as in si**ng**

ng·g - as in a**ng**ry

nk - as in i**nk**

p - as in **p**ut

r - as in **r**an

s - as in **s**it

sh - as in **sh**e

t - as in **t**o

th - as in brea**the**

th - th as in brea**th**

v - as in **v**ery

w - as in **w**in

y - as in **y**es

z - as in **z**oo

zh - as in mea**s**ure

Vowels

a - as in b**a**t

ä - as in c**a**r

ā - as in c**a**re

ā - as in l**a**te

â - as in t**a**ll

aû - as in **ow**l

ė - as in b**e**

e - as in b**e**t

ē - as in f**ee**t

ē - as in h**e**r

ə - as in **the**

ī - as in m**i**ne

i - as in p**i**n

o - as in g**o**t

ô - as in **o**r

ō - as in r**o**te

oo - as in m**oo**n

ū - as in c**u**te

û - as in f**u**ll

u - as in r**u**b

COM·PUT·ERS

dot con [dot kon]

n. **1.** An e-mail scam. **2.** A bogus Web site. **3.** A bad investment in a Web startup.

bi·Pod [bī·pod] ···

n. Two people sharing one iPod by using one earbud each.

da·ta·clys·m [da·tə·kli·zəm]

n. A catastrophic event causing a large loss of computer data.

Goo·gli·on [goo·glė·ən]

n. A person who uses Google to find out absolutely everything he or she does not know.

e·d·dict [ē·dikt]

n. **1.** A person addicted to e-mailing, Internet browsing, or other computer-related activities. **2.** Someone who sits at the computer way too much.

hoo·gle [hoo·gəl]·······································

n. A human search engine of random knowledge; a human Google.

jar·gon·or·rhea [jär·gə·nə·rē·ə]

n. Overbearing and obnoxious shoptalk—especially the sort that uses an excess of esoteric terminology—when used in a nonwork social setting.

lu·ser [loo·zər]

n. A pain-in-the-ass user who seems consistently unable to work out the simplest of functions.

Mac·in·trash [ma·kən·trash] ·····················
adj. Of or pertaining to anything created by Apple.
n. A person who just will not stop talking about how awesome Apple products are.

not·wor·king [not·wər·king]
adj. The default state of any and all computer hardware and connections at times of critical need.

phal·la·cy [fa·lə·sė]
n. Misrepresentation of the size of one's member on the Internet.

Sky·po [skī·pō]
n. **1.** A call made by accident using Skype. **2.** A Skype call to the wrong person. **3.** A typo in a Skype chat.

spam do·nor [spam dō·nôr]
n. Someone who clogs your e-mail inbox with chain letters, Internet "specials," bad jokes, sick child pleas, doctored photos, and other completely useless junk mail.

OF·FICE

a·na·lize [ā·nəl·īz]

v. t. To assess a situation with anal-retentive attention to detail.

ass·mo·sis [as·mō·səs]

n. the process by which some people seem to succeed and advance by kissing up to the boss rather than working hard.

beep·i·lep·sy [bēp·ə·lep·sė]

n. A chronic communication disorder in which a person suddenly stops in mid-sentence to make a contorted, spastic expression while looking at a vibrating beeper or PDA, then completes the sentence as if nothing happened.

blame·storm [blām·stôrm] ·

v. i. To sit around in a group and discuss why a deadline was missed or a project failed, and who is responsible.

bos·si·nine [bôs·ə·nīn]
adj. Ridiculous and foolish, as in behavior of administrators and other office bigwigs.

cli·en·tool [klī·ən·tool]
n. A business associate you want to hit with a wrench.

con·nec·tile dys·func·tion
[kə·nek·tīl dis·funk·shən]
n. A sudden loss of Internet access, resulting in disappointment and anxiety.

cool·league [koo·lēg]
n. One of the great people you work with.

con·slu·tant [kən·slət·ənt]
n. A person who promiscuously gives expert or professional advice.

day·ca·tion [dā·kā·shən]
n. A great one-day break from the office grind, filled with one's favorite activities.

con·slu·tant

ditz·krieg [dits·krēg]

n. The onslaught of lamebrains, morons, and dim bulbs in any environment. Especially prevalent in offices, where meetings may quickly devolve into gossip, whining, and other blather.

mar·ke·tec·ture [mär·kə·tek·chər]

n. A diagram of a technical solution used in selling to nontechnical buyers.

re·su·may·be [re·zə·mā·bė]

n. A short, mostly fictitious account of one's career and qualifications, typically prepared by an applicant woefully unqualified for the position.

tel·e·mar·tyr [te·lə·mär·tər]

n. A telemarketer so persistent and annoying that he/she sacrifices all personal dignity for the benefit of a product or company.

vol·un·turd [vo·lən·tėrd]

n. One who repeatedly volunteers for things and then backs out at the last minute.

COR·PO·RATE
A·MER·I·CA

bil·li·ous [bil·é·əs]
adj. Feeling ill when there are too many bills to pay all
at once.

bir·ken·schlock [bər·kən·shläk] ················
n. Cheap or inferior goods, generally either tie-dyed
or made of hemp, sold to hippies at music festivals,
political rallies, etc.

bro·rate [brō·rāt]
v. i. To provide a wholesale rate or give a significant
discount based on friendship among men.

com·mod·i·tease [kə·mo·də·tēz]
n. A product everyone wants but no one can get.

di·stor·i·en·ta·tion
[di·stôr·é·ən·tā·shən]
n. The experience of entering a "big box" store like
Home Depot or Walmart in a new location where
everything seems familiar but the layout and floor plan
are different than what you expected.

en·e·mize [e·nə·mīz]

v. t. To turn your allies against you; to make enemies out of your friends.

gross ear·nings [grōs ər·ningz] ················

n. Money made by doing disgusting things.

ma·li·cious com·pli·ance
[mə·li·shəs kəm·plī·əns]

n. The act of performing whatever task is required, even with the knowledge that doing so will ultimately result in undesired and unintended consequences for the person who requested that the task be performed.

mas·tu·re·ba·tion [mas·tər·rē·bā·shən]

n. The self-satisfying act of trying to redeem a product-rebate offer; rarely results in ecashulation.

POL·I·TICS

ad·hoc·ra·cy [ad·hok·rə·sė]

n. The result of a government that continually slaps on new agencies and programs in response to perceived threats, problems, crises, and other issues.

air·u·dite [ār·yə·dīt]

adj. Demonstrating an appalling lack of common sense that frequently occurs among people who have achieved advanced academic degrees.

Al·gore·a·pho·bi·a [al·gôr·ə·fō·bė·ə]

n. The irrational fear of Al Gore.

be·ne·vi·o·lence [bə·ne·vī·ə·ləns] ··············

n. The astounding use of destructive means to achieve noble goals.

Bushed [bûsht]

adj. **1.** Stupefied by George W. Bush. **2.** Temporarily afflicted with idiocy while trying to understand and/or accept Bush's policies.

Bu·shit [bû·shit]

n. [Self-explanatory.]

con·glom·mon·wealth
[kən·glô·mən·welth]

n. The new corporate-colonial government that the United States and its allies are setting up in Iraq.

crit·i·zen [krit·ə·zən]

n. A legally recognized national of a state or commonwealth who thinks and responds critically, sometimes vehemently, to the statements or actions of elected representatives and government officials. *See also* blogger.

flag·whore [flag·hôr]·················

n. A person who thinks sticking an American flag on every possible surface is the only way to be patriotic.

flex·i·bull [flek·sə·bûl]

adj. Easily switching from one line of BS to another.

4

for·eign fal·la·cy [fôr·ən fa·lə·sė]
n. The idea that some people are foreign and need to be dealt with through a specific policy.

gov·ern·meant [go·vərn·ment]
n. What the United States government was designed to be before a small group of wealthy men turned it into a domestic extortion operation and an international terror.

in·ter·ror·ga·tion [in·ter·ər·ga·shən]
n. A new standard of interrogation—in violation of the Geneva Convention—only performed on terror suspects.

jus·ti·fic·tion [jus·tə·fik·shən]
n. **1.** Creative justification. **2.** Hypocritical justice, which differs according to political application.

pret·ze·lize [pret·sə·līz]
v. t. To contort a simple piece of linear logic into an obtuse and needlessly complex explanation.

rep·re·hens·a·tive [re·pri·hen·sə·tiv]

n. A member of the lower house of Congress; capitalized when used as a title.

Re·pub·li·can't [ri·pu·bli·kant]

n. A normally steadfast Republican who simply cannot support any of the party's nominees.

strag·e·dy [stra·jə·dė]

n. A strategy that results in tragic consequences upon implementation.

ve·ge·ter·ro·rist [ve·jə·ter·ər·ist] ················

n. An activist whose radical vegetarian agenda persecutes innocent omnivore bystanders.

vo·ti·va·tion [vō·tə·vā·shən]

n. The primary motivator that drives a typically apathetic citizen to participate in the electoral process.

MED·I·CINE

ad·da·dict·o·my [ad·ə·dik·tə·mė]
n. A surgical procedure performed on a female patient who wants to change gender.

AM·A·zone [a·mə·zōn]
n. A place of confluence for members of the American Medical Association, such as a hospital.

ce·re·be·la·tion [sə·rə·bə·lā·shən]
n. A chemical reaction in your brain that makes you feel elated after having a good idea.

cor·pu·lint [kôr·pyə·lint] ·······························
adj. A condition of the morbidly obese characterized by an increased propensity for accumulating belly button lint.

cra·ni·al·rec·tu·mi·tis
[krā·nė·əl·rek·tə·mī·təs]
n. A common medical condition where one's head is up one's ass. This condition is usually accompanied by a false sense of security and delusions of grandeur.

heal·thi·tize [hel·thə·tīz]
v. t. To make an otherwise unhealthy food look healthy by fortifying it with vitamins and minerals.

lac·tard [lak·tärd]
n. A politically incorrect term for a lactose-intolerant person.

on·call·o·gist [ôn·kâ·lə·jist]
n. A doctor who is on call all the time.

pre·tend·o·ni·tis [prē·tend·ə·nī·təs]
n. A condition suffered by hypochondriacs.

scribb·la·ture [skrib·lə·tyûr]
n. **1.** The act of writing one's name illegibly, especially in the medical profession. **2.** An illegible signature, especially one confirming identity, as on a credit card receipt.

PUBS & CLUBS

al·co·hol·ler [al·kə·hol·ər]
n. The sound of a loud drunk.

bar hum·bug [bär hum·bug]
n. The early-morning remorse of an overenthusiastic drinker.

beer·va·na [bēr·vä·nə]···························
n. A blissful state of being oblivious to pain, reached through copious consumption of beer.

drun·kle [drun·kəl]
n. A member of one's extended family who has too much to drink at almost every single family function.

for·ni·ca·to·ri·um [fôr·ni·kə·tôr·ė·əm]
n. A place where people gather at night to drink and hang out, often leading to yadda yadda. Often refers to the home or apartment of a group of singles who frequently host such gatherings, but can also be a bar, pub, or nightclub.

mock·tail [mok·tāl]
n. A nonalcoholic drink that looks and acts like a cocktail.

pre·ma·ture e·ta·pu·la·tion [pri·mə·tyûr i·ta·pyə·lā·shən]
n. The act of tapping a keg of beer prior to the beginning of the party, often resulting in early depletion of said beer.

smar·ti·ni [smär·tē·nė]
n. A cocktail that makes you believe you have something genius to say after copious consumption.

swig·ger [swi·gər]
n. A gait peculiar to one who is simultaneously perambulating and taking sips from a bottle in a paper bag.

u·ti·ni [yoo·tē·nė]
n. A martini served in Utah: tiny, containing very little alcohol.

LI·TE·RA·TI

ac·ro·nym·ese [ak·rə·nim·ēz]
n. A dialect characterized by too many acronyms.

a·glyph·i·cate [ə·glif·ə·kāt]
v. i. To avoid or put off a writing assignment until the last possible moment.

eard [ĕrd] ···
v. t. To listen to an audio book.

el·lam·en·o·pee [el·em·en·ō·pē]
n. An often slurred, muddled, and corrupted series of letters from the English alphabet, consisting of L, M, N, O, and P.

ex·treme Scrab·ble [ik·strēm skra·bəl]
n. An unsanctioned version of the board game in which the only criterion of validity for a word is the ability of the player to convince a majority of other players that the word (a) exists and (b) means what he/she says it means.

Jane Aus·tis·m [jān ôs·ti·zəm]
n. Malady associated with the annoying habit of
constantly quoting from *Pride and Prejudice*, *Emma*,
Sense and Sensibility, etc.

lex·e·cu·tion·er [lek·sə·kū·shə·nər]··········
n. One who has a particular knack for butchering
language.

O·prah·size [ō·prə·sīz]
v. t. To promote undue adulation for a book of
mediocre literary substance.

Shake·spare [shāk·spãr]
n. The abridged *Bard for Dummies*.

T-squire [tē·skwīr]
n. An author whose work is published on T-shirts;
abbreviated "Tsq."

werd [wẽrd]
n. A made-up word.

SPORTS

8

base·brawl [bās·brôl]

n. A violent game of baseball.

bi·pass [bī·pas]

n. The act of running past someone, only to be over-taken so that you must pass a second time.

fore·scythe [fôr·sīth]

v. t. To reap grass with a golf club.

fore·site [fôr·sīt]

n. The location where a golf spectator has been hit by a ball in flight.

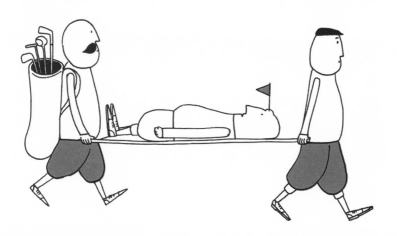

8

KEEP
OFF THE
GRASS

jock·ass [jôk·as]

n. An egotistical son-of-a-bitch who believes his God-given talent to play games gives him the right to act like a total jerk.

out·doork [aût·dôrk]

n. A person who takes the outdoor lifestyle very seriously in order to appear "extreme" or overly adventurous.

sho·gul [shō·gəl]

v. i. To ski moguls with the precision and vigor of a feudal Japanese governor.

sigh·at·i·ca [sī·a·ti·kə]

n. Resignation to missing a race due to sciatic nerve pain.

snot·si·cle [snot·si·kəl]

n. A drip of snot that hangs off your nose on a cold day.

two-foot flu [too·fût floo]

n. The condition an employee has after it has snowed more than two feet.

un·der·dog·ging [un·dər·dâg·ing]

n. The tendency to almost invariably side with the underdog in any situation.

8

RE·LI·GION
&
PHI·LOS·O·PHY

ag·nos·to·hol·ic [ag·nos·tə·hô·lik]

n. One who takes an "I'll believe it when I see it" attitude toward everything.

egg·nos·tic [eg·nos·tik] ·····················

adj. **1.** Uncertain about which came first—the chicken or the egg—but open to either someday being proved the one-and-only true progenitor. **2.** Uncertain about what to put in one's omelet.

eth·no·mas·o·chis·m
[eth·nō·ma·sə·ki·zəm]

n. Disgust with one's own ethnic group, especially when its members act out perceived stereotypes.

e·vil·u·tion [ē·vəl·oo·shən]

n. What the Religious Right wants you to believe.

e·vil·u·tion

fool·os·o·phy [fool·o·sə·fė]
n. A stupid ideology.

L. Ron Hub·tard [el ron hub·tärd] · · · · · · · · · · · ·
n. A Scientologist.

la·men·ta·li·ty [lə·men·ta·lə·tė]
n. A sorrowful or mournful attitude toward life.

me·al·i·ty [mē·a·lə·tė]
n. **1.** The quality or state of being me. **2.** A thing that
exists solely for the benefit of me.

o·va·ry to·wer [ō·və·rė taû·ər]
n. A university hamstrung by radical feminism.

phi·los·o·phi·ckle [fi·lo·sə·fi·kəl]
adj. Changing one's fundamental outlook on life and nature frequently, with little thought.

pres·age·ist [pre·sij·ist]
n. One who, upon entering the next decade, predicts that his/her life is over, and that this decade will be his/her last.

proc·to·vi·sio·na·ry
[prok·to·vi·zhə·ner·ė]
adj. Looking at the world with one's head up one's ass.

rai·cist [rā·zist]
n. A person with a prejudice against dried fruit, especially raisins.

rect·oph·thal·mi·a [rek·tof·thal·mė·ə]
n. A condition resulting from the fusion of the rectal and optic nerves, giving the sufferer a crappy outlook on life.

9

re·lig·ish [rē·li·jish]

adj. No longer believing in the dogma with which
one was raised, but still feigning belief and feeling
obliged to participate, albeit halfheartedly, in religious
activities.

ser·en·dig·gi·dy [ser·ən·di·gə·dė]

n. A happy accident resulting in much dopeness; an
unanticipated but very fresh turn of events; a fortunate
coincidizzle.

skep·ti·cles [skep·ti·kəls]

n. Eyewear that causes the user to lean toward disbelief
of any new ideas or information; the opposite of rose-
colored glasses.

zen·vy [zen·vė]

n. The feeling one gets when meeting someone more
spiritual than oneself.

TRAV·EL

brief·case bling [brēf·kās bling]
n. The collection of frequent-flyer gold cards in one's briefcase.

car·bage [kär·bij]
n. The sort of trash often found on the floor and under the seats of an automobile, e.g., newspapers, maps, soda cans, crumbs, wrappers, etc.

car·co·pho·ny [kär·ka·fə·nė]
n. The din of arguing or playing children in the back of a car.

clan·des·ti·na·tion
[klan·des·tə·nā·shən]
n. **1.** A secret stopover on a trip. **2.** A vacation hideaway. **3.** A country so hidden no one can find it.

in·con·ti·nen·tal [in·kon·tə·nen·təl] · · · · · · · · · · · ·
adj. Suffering from digestive dysfunction as a result of travel in foreign lands.

lei·sure·o·lo·gist [lē·zhur·o·lə·jist]

n. An individual in constant pursuit of leisure activities; often gives advice to others on how best to spend leisure time.

man·ly·van [man·lē·van]··

n. A compact vehicle, sometimes mistaken for a minivan, only operated by an often disgruntled male driver. Often found at sporting venues, electronics stores, and establishments that serve alcohol.

nag·i·va·tor [nag·ə·vā·tər]

n. A person in charge of reading the map or directions and telling the driver which way to go and how to execute said directions.

poor·sche [pôr·schə]

n. The car you drive when you can't afford a Porsche.

ride·zil·la [rīd·zi·lə] ·····························
n. A woman who becomes a monster as soon as she gets behind the wheel of a car.

Rwan·da·lust [roo·än·dä·lust]
n. A burning desire to travel to Rwanda.

som·nam·bu·lance [som·nam·byoo·lans]
n. A moving vehicle operated by a sleeping driver.

stew·ard·ass [stoo·ērd·as]
n. A flight attendant who is overly serious and relishes in harassing passengers to enforce pointless regulations.

trip·i·da·tion [trip·ə·dā·shən]

n. A state of alarm or dread that your vacation is coming to an end.

trev·el·er [tre·və·lĕr]

n. A person who tours the world in unending search of good times.

Vi·ag·ra Falls [vī·a·grə fâls]

n. A honeymoon getaway where newlyweds never leave their hotel rooms.

FOOD
&
DRINK

brew·tal [broo·təl] ··························

n. Coffee so strong that it instantly gets one wired.

carb·e·ra·tor [kärb·i·rā·tər]

n. One who gives another a hard time for eating carbohydrates.

ce·re·al of·fend·er [sir·é·əl ə·fend·ər]

n. A person who takes an item off the shelf in a grocery store, then later decides to discard it on a random shelf elsewhere in the store. *Syn.* shopdrifter

crap·puc·ci·no [krap·ə·chē·nō]

n. A very poor cup of coffee.

de·men·tos [di·men·tōs]

n. The sticky, amorphous remains of a roll of mints, discovered in the pocket of a jacket that hasn't been worn for several months.

de·svelte [dē·svelt]
n. The process by which a diet—and one's figure—goes to hell.

fat·kins di·et [fat·kinz dī·ət]
n. A meat-based diet that obese children who never exercise are put on in the hope that they will become productive members of society.

Fri·to·lay·shun [frē·tō·lā·shən]
n. The process of shaking a bag of snacks to make the larger ones rise to the top.

gas·tro·gas·m [gas·trō·ga·zəm]
n. The eruptive psychotropic event resulting from a sudden and intense gastronomic experience, usually accompanied by a guttural vocalization.

ham·bug·ger·ed [ham·bu·gĕrd]
adj. Addicted to McDonald's to such an extent that one's health is now utterly screwed.

han·gry [hang·grė]···

adj. Hungry to the point of anger.

in·del·i·ca·tes·sen [in·de·li·kə·te·sən]

n. An eating establishment where bad table manners are not only tolerated, but encouraged and commonly practiced.

man·o·rex·i·a [man·ə·rek·sė·ə]

n. A condition among men who obsessively watch their weights and figures. Symptoms include carb counting, salad eating, frequent trips to the scale, and an unnatural knowledge of one's weight at any given moment.

perk·a·to·ry [pərk·ə·tôr·ė]

n. The period spent waiting for one's first cup of coffee in the morning.

pi·not e·gri·gi·o [pi·nō ē·gri·jē·ō]
n. A white wine of exceptionally poor quality and/or high price.

Red·bul·ly [red·bû·lė]
n. A person so wired on Red Bull that he/she turns into a raging bull over the simplest perceived slight.

vend·e·te·ri·a [vend·ə·tir·ė·ə]
n. A cafeteria consisting of a collection of vending machines.

walk·o [wâ·kō]
n. The act of eating a taco on the go.

OLIVES

CRAB BISQUE
SOUP
①

WOOD PIGEON
①
RARE   MEDIUM   CHAR
○   ○   ○

SAUTÉED
FOIE GRAS
○○ ①

STEAK
TARTARE

ORGANIC
POACHED TROUT
○○ ① □

GRAVY
①○   □
THICK   THIN

ZUCCHINI
RISOTTO
① ○○

BAKED
ALASKA
DELICIOUS!
○○①

CRÈME
BRULÉE

CHEESE
BOARD
○ ①

ESPRESSO
S M L
○ ○ ○
①

MINTS
①

11

HOL·LY·WOOD

THEATER

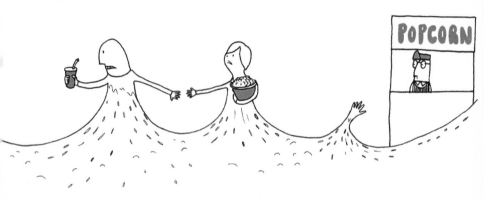

bling·a·list [bling·ə·list]

n. **1.** One who wears tons of bling, to the point of distraction. **2.** One who studies the art of bling-wearing.

ci·ne·muck [si·nə·muk]

n. The nasty, gooey, indescribable stuff on the floor at the movie theater.

co·mi·car·cass [ko·mi·kär·kəs]

n. A comedian who crashes and burns during a performance.

crock·u·men·ta·ry [krok·yū·men·tə·rė]

n. A film or video that presents incorrect or unsubstantiated allegations as proved fact.

dol·lup·tu·ous [dô·ləp·shə·wəs]
adj. Having an unrealistically proportioned figure.

five·sha·dow·ing [fiv·sha·dō·ing]
n. An extremely predictable plotline.

ir·ri·tain·ment [ir·ə·tān·mənt]
n. Media spectacles that are annoying, but you cannot stop watching.

man·scap·ing [man·skāp·ing]········
n. Male grooming.

ma·tri·mo·ney [ma·trə·mu·nė]
n. The act of marrying for money.

Par·is·ite [par·is·īt]
n. A paparazzo or person who consumes his or her time with the foibles of Paris Hilton.

pro·sti·tot [pros·tə·tot] ························
n. A teen or tween who follows in the footsteps of celebrity bad girls such as Britney Spears, Paris Hilton, etc.

scan·da·la·bra [skan·dəl·ä·brə]
n. Undergarment, often worn by certain models or actresses, that leaves nothing to the imagination.

Spiel·burb [spēl·bĕrb]
n. A bleak, monochromatic (typically beige) suburban tract, akin to those frequently depicted in Steven Spielberg movies.

FAM·I·LY

ba·do·le·scent [bad·ə·le·sənt]
n. A misbehaving teenager.

crule [krool]
n. A rule so nonsensical that it is cruel to apply it and painful to obey it.

ig·no·wrench [ig·nə·rench]··
n. The state of not knowing one tool from another.

ma·ma·fi·a [mä·mä·fė·ə]
n. An organization of overzealous mothers who intimidate principals and rule the roost.

mom·i·tize [mäm·ə·tīz]
v. t. To brainwash others into mothering children that aren't even theirs.

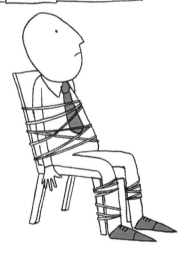

ma·ma·fi·a

mom·ni·vore [mäm·ni·vôr] ·····················

n. **1.** A child who will eat anything his/her mother puts on the table. **2.** A five-year-old still begging for mother's milk.

mom·op·o·ly [mä·mä·pə·lė]

n. A large gathering of moms who talk excessively about their children.

mom·u·ment [mäm·yə·ment]

n. **1.** The real meaning of Mom's advice. **2.** A statue commemorating motherhood.

nip·ple·tis·m [ni·pəl·ti·zəm]

n. When parents allow their children to remain on the financial "teat."

pro·tax·i·na·tor [prō·taks·ə·nā·tər]

n. A spouse who ignores the tax-related expenses of his/her sole proprietorship until April 14. Every year.

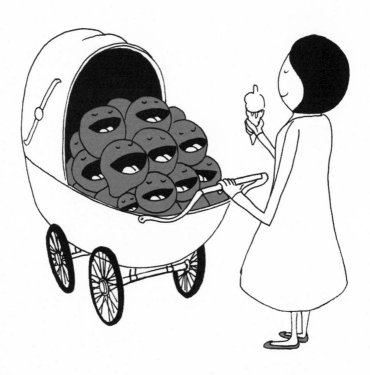

re·ju·ve·na·li·a [rė·joo·və·nā·lė·ə]
n. All the products found in the beauty and antiaging aisle of the pharmacy.

she·had [shē·häd]
n. A holy war undertaken by one's wife when one has really screwed up.

steam·strol·lered [stēm·strō·lėrd]··············
adj. Forced to leave the footpath by a collection of mothers with strollers.

strol·ler·i·za·tion [strōl·er·ə·zā·shən]
n. The polarization that occurs between women friends when one of them has a baby.

sub·rub [sub·rub]
n. Suburban massage parlor.

tes·tos·ter·zone [tes·tos·tər·zōn]

n. The area surrounding any gathering of men with no women present, often accompanied by the presence of cigar smoke.

was·band [wuz·bənd]

n. A man who was your husband.

zooom [zooom]

v. i. To zip through a zoo and see as many animals as possible in a very short amount of time.

PETS
&
OTH·ER AN·I·MALS

a·ro·ma·dil·lo [ar·rō·mä·di·lō]

n. An armadillo in the early stages of putrefaction, especially one rolled upon by your dog.

ass·quack [as·kwak]··

n. A strange fart that sounds like the call of a duck or goose.

Beel·ze·bug [bē·el·zi·bug]

n. Satan in the form of a mosquito that gets into the bedroom at three in the morning and cannot be cast out.

bit·map [bit·map]

n. A map rescued from the dog a moment too late.

cat·i·quette [kat·i·ket]

n. The proper rules of engagement when dealing with felines.

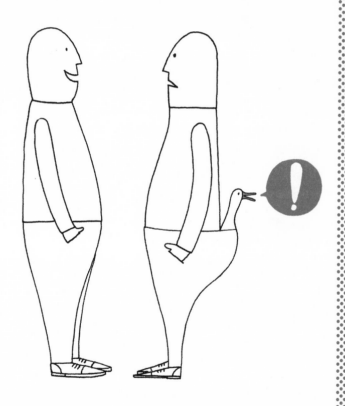

dé·jà moo [dā·zhä moo]

n. The feeling that you have heard this bull before.

don·ku·bine [däng·kyū·bīn]··················

n. A mistress who looks like a farm animal.

dra·ma·dar·y [drä·mə·de·rė]

n. A histrionic camel.

fur·play [fĕr·plā]

n. The amorous actions between furry woodland creatures before the act of mating.

gi·raff [ja·raf]

n. A male giraffe; note the missing "e."

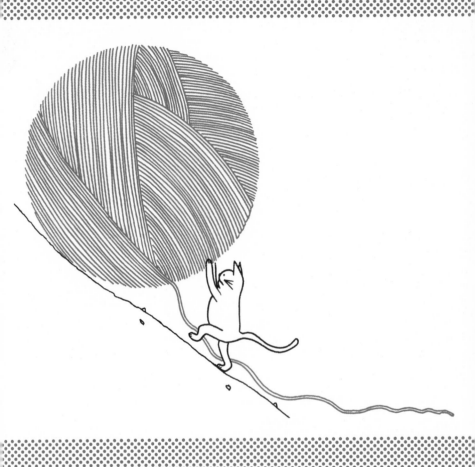

im·pet·i·ment [im·pe·tə·mənt]

n. A dog, cat, or other pet that interferes with one's ability to do something, such as travel, buy new things, or have relations with one's partner.

poop·si·cle [poop·si·kəl]

n. Frozen excrement.

psy·cho·phant [sī·kō·fənt]

n. A seriously disturbed pachyderm.

pug·ger·naut [pug·ər·nât]

n. A small dog that destroys everything in its path and simply cannot be stopped.

sis·y·puss [si·sə·pûs]

n. A cat that is damned to push a boulder up a hill for eternity.

DAT·ING
&
SEX·U·AL·I·TY

a·man·i·ty [ə·man·ə·tė]

n. A man who is pleasant, agreeable, and who provides sexual comforts and conveniences for the woman in his life.

as·sass [a·sas]

v. t. To determine the quality of a gluteus maximus.

blue blahs [bloo bläz]

n. The condition of really needing to get laid but being too depressed to do anything about it.

bor·ny [bôr·nė]

adj. Bored and horny.

bro·mance [brō·mans]

n. The heterosexual relationship between two men who are together constantly.

bus·y·baw·dy [bi·zė·bô·dė]
n. A person who loves you and sneaks through your
e-mail looking for evidence of infidelity and other
degenerate behavior.

clea·ver·age [klē·və·rij]
n. The power that women with large breasts possess
over society.
v. t. To affect a man's decision-making process by
wearing a low-cut dress.

e·pooph·any [i·poof·a·ny] ·····················
n. The sudden realization that one might be gay.

hor·ny·mone [hôr·nė·mōn]
n. A biological chemical often credited with the
onset of pubescent interest in the opposite sex.

man·ki·ni [man·kē·nė]
n. A brief swimming costume worn by men,
epitomized by the over-the-shoulder "ball cup"
holder worn by Borat.

man·thrax [man·thraks]
n. A man who is bad for you, or who has treated you badly.

mas·sag·y·nist [mə·säzh·ə·nist]
n. One who hates to massage women; one who will only massage men.

mul·ti·ple sar·cas·ms [mul·tə·pəl sär·ka·zəmz]
n. pl. The feeble attempts by men to save face after a woman says she faked multiple orgasms.

nar·ci·sex·u·al [när·si·sek·shə·wəl]
adj. Attracted to oneself.

plu·ton·ic [ploo·to·nik]
adj. Describes a relationship that could, or should, only exist in outer space.

queer·i·ous [kwir·é·əs]

adj. Cautiously probing with respect to another's sexual orientation.

que·ry of rel·a·tiv·i·ty ·
[kwir·é ov rel·ə·tiv·ə·té]

n. Asking one's mother if a hot cousin is really a cousin, or if one of you is adopted.

sin·er·gy [sin·ər·jé]

n. Two or more people creating more sin than just one person alone.

va·gel·lan [və·je·lən]

n. An explorer in search of a woman's G-spot.
v. To go in search of a woman's G-spot.

vag·e·tar·i·an [vaj·ə·ter·é·ən]

n. One whose sexuality is a strict diet of women.

FUN
&
GAMES

chro·ni·cide [krō·nə·sīd]
n. The killing of time.

naht·zee [nät·sė]
n. One who displays a manic zeal for dice games, particularly Yahtzee.

screw·phor·i·a [skroo·fôr·ė·ə]
n. The elation that one feels when an enemy is vanquished (or at least annoyed).

Wii·flex [wē·fleks] ·
n. The special dexterity needed to respond to games played on the Wii console.

Wii·tard [wē·tärd]
n. One who cannot manage to hold onto a Wiimote, let alone use it properly.

WoW·o·ver [waû·ō·vər]
n. The feeling that follows a sixteen-hour *World of Warcraft* session.

WORDS THAT
AL·MOST EX·IST

as·sas·sin' [a·sas·in]
coll. Sassing. Used, with subtly different inflections, in Italy and the southern United States.

awk·weird [âk·wird]
adj. Equal parts awkward and weird.

bend·er·pho·bi·a [ben·dər·fõ·bė·ə]
n. **1.** A fear of bending over. **2.** When capitalized, a fear of animated robots.

bru·ta·ful [broo·tə·fəl]
adj. Either brutal or beautiful, depending upon one's vantage point.

cal·en·drome [ka·lən·drōm]
n. A date or year that reads the same both ways.

con·flic·ti·pa·ted [kən·flik·tə·pā·təd]··········
adj. Seriously unable to make a decision due to too many choices; indecisive to the point of pain.

con·ver·sua·sion [kän·vər·swā·zhən] ··········
n. A conversation held for the purpose of persuasion.

di·le·ma·ma [də·le·mä·mä]
n. The mother of all dilemmas.

eb·la·bo·rate [i·blab·ə·rāt]
v. t. To add further and often superfluous details in an indiscreet and thoughtlessly chatty manner.

fac·tate [fak·tāt]
v. i. **1.** To spew facts. **2.** To act like one knows it all.

fac·ti·tious [fak·ti·shəs]
adj. Real; substantial; based in fact.

fa·stu·di·ous [fa·stoo·dė·əs]
adj. Quick to master academic subjects.

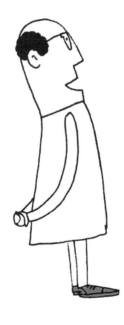

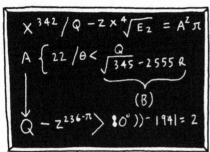

$$X^{342} / Q - Z \times \sqrt[4]{E_2} = A^2 \pi$$

$$A \left\{ 22 / \theta < \underbrace{\frac{Q}{\sqrt{345} - 2555 R}} \right.$$

$$(B)$$

$$Q - Z^{236 \cdot \pi} > 80°)) - 1941 = 2$$

fa·stu·di·ous

fla·cet [fla·sət]
n. An aspect of one's multidimensional character that is weak or underdeveloped.

fri·vi·al [fri·vė·əl]
adj. Frivolous and trivial.

gri·nace [gri·nəs]
n. A facial expression showing the combination of a smile and a frown that can occur when opening an undesirable present or meeting a blind date. Betrays the battle between the mores of polite society and the real feelings that lurk beneath.

in·un·ten·tion·al [in·ən·ten·shə·nəl]
adj. Accidentally on purpose.

per·haps·i·bly [pėr·hap·sə·blė]
adv. Plausibly.

per·taint [pėr·tānt]
v. t. To sully by association.

pre·ci·pro·cate [pri·si·prə·kāt]
v. t. To do a small favor in anticipation of receiving an
even bigger favor in return.

sar·cas·ti·gate [sär·kas·tə·gāt]
v. t. To censure severely with sarcasm.

sat·is·fac·tu·al [sa·təs·fak·choo·əl]
adj. Factual enough.

sort·ga·nize [sôrt·gə·nīz]
v. t. To sort and organize in a heightened mental state.

te·le·pa·the·tic [te·lə·pə·the·tik]
adj. Characteristic of the inappropriate laughter of one
or more persons following a shared dumb interpreta-
tion of a situation.

ye·ses·sa·ri·ly [yes·ə·ser·ə·lė]
adv. The argumentative counter to the statement
"Not necessarily."

MIS·CEL·LA·NEOUS

18

bab·be·li·cious [ba·bə·li·shəs]
adj. Particularly juicy, pertaining to a speech that one wishes would not end.

col·lid·o·scope [kə·lī·də·skōp]
n. A zoom function on a camera, used to take pictures at car-crash scenes.

cri·min·i·mal [kri·mi·nə·məl]··················
n. A thief whose acquisitions are small enough not to be missed or even noticed by the original owners.

dis·tink·tive [di·stink·tiv]
adj. Of or relating to a unique individual odor.

du·op·o·ly [doo·o·pə·lė]
n. Twins in sync.

gi·raf·fi·ti [jə·ra·fẽ·tė]

n. Vandalism spray-painted very, very high up.

hat·i·tudes [hat·ə·toodz]

n. Kentucky Derby attendees strutting around Churchill Downs wearing their big hats.

him·mi·cane [him·ə·kān]

n. 1. A male hurricane. 2. A hurricane with a man's name.

18

ig·no·ra·nus [ig·na·rā·nus]

n. A person who is both stupid and an asshole.

sar·chasm [sar·ka·zam]

n. The gulf between the author of sarcastic wit and the person who doesn't get it.

self·one [self·ōn] ·····································

v. i. To borrow someone else's telephone to call your lost cell phone.

sleeve·zure [slēv·zhər]

n. A body convulsion resulting from getting one's arm caught in the sleeve while removing one's shirt.

win·dow pain [win·dō pān]

n. The pain felt when walking full-speed into a really clean sliding glass door or plate glass window.

Acknowledgments

The Addictionary (at home on the Web at www.addictionaries.com) is for word lovers—those neologists who help our beloved English language grow in both serious and humorous ways. Most of us have been making up words since we were little kids. Everyone seems to have a word or two—or two *hundred*.

We built the Addictionary to empower and enable *you* to engage in intelligent and humorous wordplay, to help you showcase and market your cleverness and creativity to the world. It's a game everyone can play; and the wordiacs, wordnerds, and addictionados have indeed responded.

We're reciprocating with the first volume of the best-of-the-best from early Addictionary contributions. We started with one word—"plutonic"—and you turned it into a growing compendium of tens of thousands of words and definitions. If you see your Addictionary username on the inside cover of this book, you made the cut as a contributor to the inaugural edition. Your lexemplary contributions have been recognized. Nice work.

Kudos to Robert Hanson, as well. An illustrator of amazing talent, he was able to educe the visual humor from your words and turn them into laugh-out-loud funny line art.

I'm also proud to acknowledge my fellow snowflakes in Park City, Utah, and all those domestic and abroad who, now or then, inspired, affected, evolved, and slaved over the Addictionary to help create the ultimate lingo engine: Robin Rankin, Kelly McCrystal, Heather Semon, Chad Tilbury, Mike Nestor, Michael Thomas, Jeff Kuehn, Junjet Trasmonte, Santiago Castillo, Whey Ragadio, Edgar Gonzalez, Basilio Bogado, Pål de Vibe, Bit Santos, Kristine Peromingan, Joe Tandingan, Grady Kelly, Jeff Lorenzen, Amy Errett, Sabrina Riddle, and Brad Lande. And the lovely folks at Abrams Image who have taken those bits and turned them into atoms chock-full of cleverness: Aiah Wieder, Alissa Faden, Leslie Stoker, Jacquie Poirier, Maxine Kaplan, and Beau Friedlander. And last, but never, ever least, our lovely and tireless agent, Jayne Rockmill.

There's more coming from the Addictionaries. Keep your eyes peeled, tongues untied, fingertips nimble, and pencils sharp.

What's your word?
www.addictionaries.com